the LLAMA SUTRA

Getting Wild in the Wild Kingdom

HYLAS

Hylas Publishing®
129 Main Street, Ste. C
Irvington, NY 10533
www.hylaspublishing.com

Hylas Publishing
Publisher: Sean Moore
Publishing Director: Karen Prince
Art Director: Gus Yoo
Designer: La Tricia Watford, Shamona Stokes, Erika Lubowicki
Editorial Director: Ward Calhoun
Photo Researcher: Benjamin DeWalt
Proofreader: Suzanne Lander

ISBN: 1-59258-257-5
ISBN 13/EAN: 978-1592-58257-0

Library of Congress Cataloging-in-Publication Data available upon request.
Printed and bound in Singapore
Distributed in the United States by Publishers Group West
Distributed in Canada by Publishers Group Canada
First American Edition published in 2006
2 4 6 8 10 9 7 5 3 1

the LLAMA SUTRA

Getting Wild in the Wild Kingdom

WARD CALHOUN

HYLAS
PUBLISHING

I think three days of foreplay is enough already.

10

In a while crocodile.

43

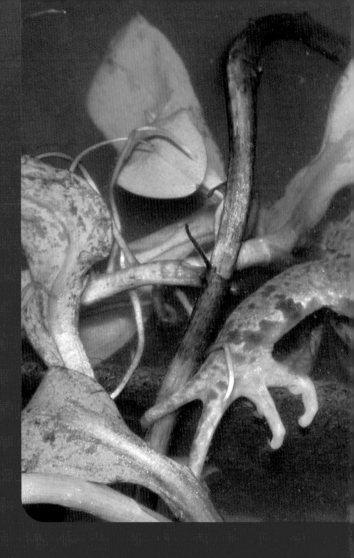

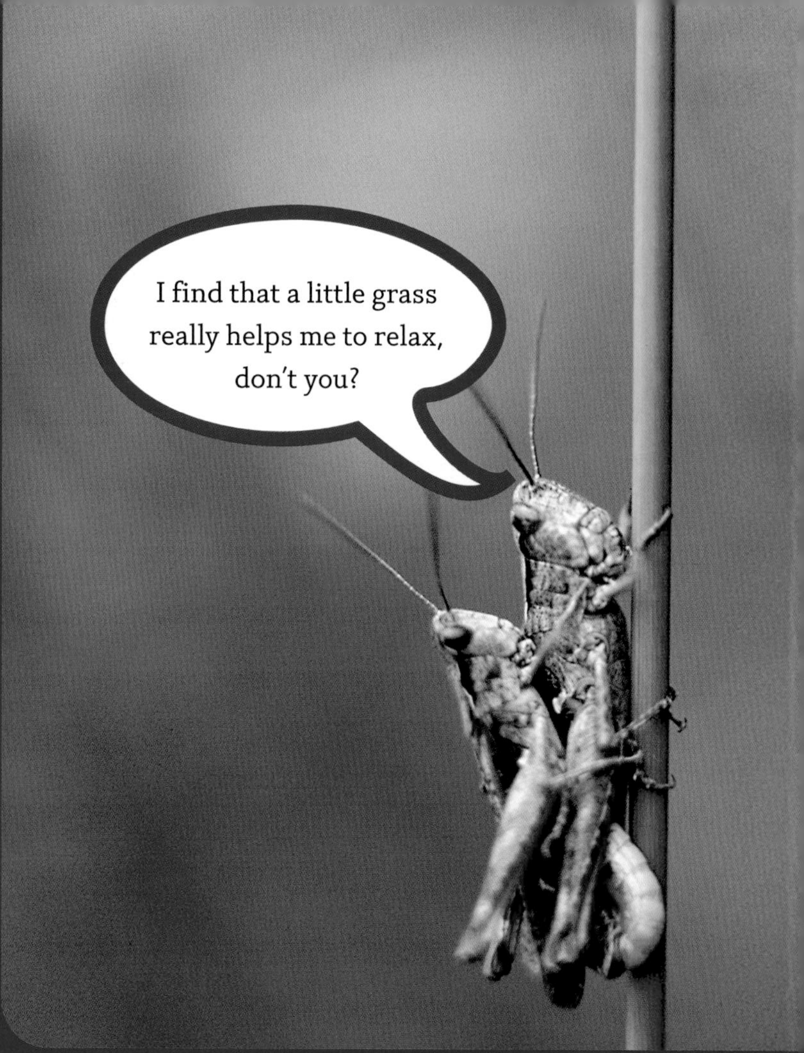
I find that a little grass really helps me to relax, don't you?